I0478082

 LESSONS FOR LASTING IMPACT

LEADERSHIP

Essential Strategies for Modern Leaders

  **LISTENING**

EMPATHY

 **ADAPTABILITY**

 **DECISIVENESS**

 **EMPOWERMENT**

 **RESILIENCE**

 **STRATEGY**

 **HUMILITY**

INTEGRITY

 **PASSION**

GAURANG PATEL

Copyright

"LEADERSHIP: Lessons for Lasting Impact - Essential Strategies for Modern Leaders to Inspire, Empower, and Succeed" by Gaurang Patel

Copyright © 2024 Gaurang Patel. All rights reserved.

No part of this book may be reproduced, distributed, or transmitted in any form or by any means, including photocopying, recording, or other electronic or mechanical methods, without the prior written permission of the author, except in the case of brief quotations embodied in critical reviews and certain other non-commercial uses permitted by copyright law.

First Edition
2024-2025

Acknowledgments

I would like to express my heartfelt gratitude to everyone who contributed to the creation of this book. First and foremost, thank you to my family and friends for their unwavering support and encouragement throughout my writing journey. Your belief in me fuelled my passion to complete this project.

I extend my gratitude to the mentors and leaders who have inspired me with their insights, lessons, and examples of effective leadership. Your teachings have profoundly shaped my understanding of what it means to lead with integrity and purpose.

I would also like to acknowledge my readers. Your desire for personal and professional growth inspires me to continue sharing knowledge and insights. I hope this book serves as a valuable resource in your leadership journey.

Finally, a special thanks to the editorial team and everyone who provided feedback on my work. Your constructive criticism and support were invaluable in refining this manuscript. Additionally, much of the text was generated with the help of AI, which has greatly assisted in the writing process.

Preface

In an ever-evolving world, the need for effective leadership has never been more pronounced. Whether in business, education, or community initiatives, leaders play a pivotal role in shaping the future and inspiring those around them. "LEADERSHIP: Lessons for Lasting Impact" aims to equip current and aspiring leaders with essential strategies to navigate the complexities of modern leadership.

This book is structured around the acronym "LEADERSHIP," with each letter representing a crucial aspect of effective leadership. From Listening to Passion, the chapters delve into the fundamental traits and skills that can empower leaders to inspire, motivate, and drive meaningful change. Through practical insights, real-life examples, and actionable strategies, readers will discover how to cultivate these essential qualities within themselves and their teams.

As you embark on this journey through the pages of this book, I encourage you to reflect on your leadership style and consider how you can implement these lessons in your own life. Leadership is not just about achieving results; it's about making a lasting impact on the lives of others.

Enjoy the journey!

Disclaimer

The information presented in this book is intended for educational purposes only. While every effort has been made to ensure the accuracy and reliability of the content, the author makes no representations or warranties of any kind regarding the completeness, accuracy, or reliability of the information contained herein. Readers are encouraged to seek professional advice and conduct their own research when implementing the strategies discussed in this book.

The author shall not be liable for any loss, damage, or injury arising from the use or reliance on any information provided in this book. By reading this book, you acknowledge that you have read this disclaimer and agree to its terms. Portions of the text were generated with the assistance of AI, which contributed to the overall content and structure of the book.

Table of Contents

1. Introduction

"Leadership is not about being in charge. It is about taking care of those in your charge." –
Simon Sinek

1.1 Introduction

In an era marked by rapid change, technological advancements, and an increasingly interconnected global economy, the essence of leadership has transformed. It is no longer confined to authority or mere decision-making. True leadership is about inspiring others, empowering teams, and creating environments that foster innovation and integrity. This book, "LEADERSHIP: Lessons for Lasting Impact," is designed as a guide for leaders in today's dynamic world who seek to make a genuine, lasting impact. Built around the acronym "LEADERSHIP," this book distils the core principles of effective leadership into ten essential chapters, each representing a key trait that leaders must master.

1.2 Overview of the Book

Each chapter in this book explores a fundamental attribute of successful leadership, organized in an easy-to-follow, thematic structure based on the letters in the word "LEADERSHIP." From listening, the cornerstone of any strong leader's skill set, to passion, the fuel that drives both leaders and their teams to new heights, these chapters provide a structured and practical approach to leadership. Each principle is paired with actionable strategies, real-world examples, and practical exercises to help readers internalize and implement these traits in their daily lives.

Introduction

Here's a breakdown of what you can expect to find in each chapter:

1. Listening: Great leaders are great listeners. In this chapter, we examine the art of active listening, where leaders not only hear but understand their team members. Listening helps leaders foster trust, gain valuable insights, and inspire loyalty. We'll also explore techniques for overcoming listening barriers and using listening as a tool for innovation.

2. Empathy: The ability to understand and connect emotionally with others is crucial in today's diverse workplace. This chapter delves into empathy's role in leadership, providing techniques for leaders to build emotional intelligence, manage tough conversations gracefully, and embrace diverse perspectives.

3. Accountability: True leaders take responsibility for their actions and decisions. In this chapter, we explore ways to foster a culture of accountability, address mistakes with integrity, and implement feedback loops that encourage continuous improvement within teams.

4. Decisiveness: Effective leaders are known for their ability to make informed decisions quickly. We'll discuss balancing intuition with data-driven approaches, assessing risks, and analyzing examples of decisive leaders who made significant impacts in their fields.

5. Empowerment: A leader's role is not to control but to empower. In this chapter, we discuss the importance of delegating with purpose, removing obstacles, and recognizing accomplishments as a way to inspire team members to reach their full potential.

6. Resilience: The journey of leadership is filled with challenges. Resilience helps leaders and their teams bounce back from setbacks stronger than before. This chapter offers strategies for developing a resilient mindset, handling crises effectively, and maintaining well-being in the face of adversity.

7. Strategy: Vision without a plan is simply a dream. Here, we dive into the importance of strategic thinking and planning, aligning goals with a vision, and adapting to change. Leaders will learn to communicate their vision effectively and utilize planning tools to bring their goals to life.

8. Humility: Humility is often overlooked in leadership, yet it's essential for creating a culture of respect and openness. This chapter encourages leaders to embrace mistakes, seek feedback, and balance confidence with humility to foster a culture of continuous learning.

9. Integrity: Leadership grounded in honesty and ethics builds lasting trust. This chapter explores the role of transparency, ethical decision-making, and how to address conflicts with integrity. Integrity not only sustains a positive culture but also strengthens an organization's foundation.

10. Passion: Passion is the driving force behind any great leader. This final chapter discusses how leaders can inspire enthusiasm within themselves and their teams, sustain motivation through challenges, and balance passion with practicality for lasting success.

1.3   Why This Book Matters

The goal of this book is to be a comprehensive guide, helping readers develop a well-rounded understanding of each critical leadership quality. These qualities are not only beneficial in a professional setting but also play a significant role in personal growth. By working through each chapter, readers will gain insights into becoming more thoughtful, inspiring, and resilient leaders, equipped to handle both the challenges and opportunities that come with leadership.

Through a blend of compelling stories, data-backed insights, and real-world examples, "LEADERSHIP: Lessons for Lasting Impact" will guide you on a journey to discover what it truly means to lead with integrity, empathy, and vision in today's complex world. This book is intended for readers at all levels, from aspiring leaders to experienced professionals, offering timeless principles that can be adapted and applied across various contexts.

Whether you are new to leadership or have years of experience, the journey through these pages is designed to not only equip you with valuable skills but to inspire a new perspective on leadership itself—one that is grounded in authenticity, service, and a commitment to creating a positive and lasting impact.

2. Listening

"Most people do not listen with the intent to understand; they listen with the intent to reply."
— Stephen R. Covey

Listening is a cornerstone of effective leadership. It's not merely about hearing words but about truly understanding and valuing what is being communicated. In a world where distractions are plentiful and communication often occurs through screens, the ability to listen actively has never been more critical. This chapter delves into the multifaceted nature of listening, emphasizing its role in fostering trust, innovation, and a positive organizational culture.

2.1 Active Listening vs. Passive Hearing

Active listening is an intentional, engaged process that goes beyond the surface level of communication. It requires the listener to be fully present, to focus on the speaker, and to process the information being conveyed. Active listening involves several key components: giving full attention to the speaker, showing that you are listening through non-verbal cues such as nodding or maintaining eye contact, and providing feedback that clarifies understanding. This practice fosters an environment where team members feel heard and respected, ultimately leading to greater collaboration and morale.

In contrast, passive hearing is a more superficial process where one might hear words without truly understanding their meaning or context. This often leads to misunderstandings and disengagement. Passive listeners might nod along or provide minimal responses, but they are not engaged in the conversation. Understanding this distinction is essential for leaders, as active listening can lead to more effective decision-making and problem-solving. By prioritizing active listening, leaders can create a culture of open communication where team members feel valued and motivated to share their thoughts and ideas.

2.2 Building Trust Through Listening

Trust is a fundamental component of effective leadership, and listening plays a crucial role in building that trust. When leaders take the time to listen actively, they signal to their team members that their opinions and experiences are valued. This fosters an environment of mutual respect, where individuals feel comfortable expressing their thoughts and concerns without fear of judgment. Building trust through listening also involves being transparent and open in communication. Leaders should provide constructive feedback and engage in two-way conversations that encourage dialogue rather than monologue.

Moreover, leaders can enhance trust by demonstrating empathy during conversations. Acknowledging the emotions and experiences of team members, even in difficult discussions, shows that a leader cares about their well-being and perspectives. When team members feel trusted and supported, they are more likely to engage fully and contribute positively to the team's objectives. Ultimately, listening becomes a powerful tool for leaders to cultivate a culture of trust that underpins effective collaboration and team dynamics.

2.3   Techniques for Active Listening

Implementing effective techniques for active listening is essential for leaders who wish to enhance their communication skills and foster a productive environment. One key technique is reflective listening, where the listener paraphrases what the speaker has said to confirm understanding. This not only shows that the leader is engaged but also allows for any misunderstandings to be clarified on the spot. For example, a leader might say, "So what I hear you saying is that you're feeling overwhelmed with the current project timeline, correct?" This approach encourages open dialogue and reassures the speaker that their concerns are being taken seriously.

Another effective technique is to practice open-ended questioning. Instead of asking questions that can be answered with a simple "yes" or "no," leaders should encourage deeper discussion by posing questions that require more elaboration. For instance, asking "What are some challenges you foresee in this project?" invites team members to share their thoughts and concerns, promoting a richer conversation. Moreover, leaders should minimize distractions during discussions by putting away electronic devices and maintaining eye contact, which reinforces the importance of the conversation and encourages the speaker to share more freely.

Additionally, summarizing is a vital technique for ensuring that both the speaker and listener are aligned. At the end of a discussion, a leader can summarize the main points covered and agree on the next steps, thereby ensuring that everyone is on the same page. This reinforces the value of the conversation and demonstrates that the leader is committed to following through on the discussed actions.

2.4   Overcoming Listening Barriers

While active listening is a powerful tool for leaders, several barriers can impede effective listening. One common barrier is personal biases. When leaders hold preconceived notions about a person or a topic, it can colour their interpretation of the conversation. To overcome this, leaders should strive to approach each conversation with an open mind, setting aside judgments to fully understand the speaker's perspective. This can be cultivated through self-awareness and by recognizing one's biases before engaging in discussions.

Another significant barrier is environmental distractions. In a fast-paced work environment, background noise, interruptions, and multitasking can hinder active listening. Leaders can create a conducive listening environment by choosing quiet spaces for important conversations and designating specific times for discussions without interruptions.

Additionally, emotional reactions can also act as barriers to listening. If a leader feels defensive or angry about a point being discussed, it can be challenging to fully engage with the speaker. Leaders should practice emotional regulation techniques, such as deep breathing or pausing before responding, to manage their reactions and remain open during conversations. By recognizing and addressing these barriers, leaders can significantly enhance their listening skills, leading to better communication and stronger team dynamics.

2.5   Listening as a Tool for Innovation

Listening is not only essential for fostering relationships but also serves as a powerful tool for driving innovation within organizations. When leaders create a culture of active listening, they empower their team members to share their ideas freely, leading to a wealth of creative solutions and innovative approaches. Encouraging an open exchange of ideas allows organizations to harness diverse perspectives, which is particularly important in today's rapidly evolving business landscape.

One-way leaders can utilize listening as a tool for innovation is by implementing brainstorming sessions that prioritize open dialogue. In these sessions, leaders can encourage team members to voice their thoughts without fear of criticism. By establishing a "no bad ideas" policy, leaders create a safe space where individuals feel encouraged to share even the most unconventional concepts. This approach not only sparks creativity but also demonstrates to team members that their input is valued, reinforcing a sense of belonging and investment in the organization's goals.

Additionally, feedback loops can be instrumental in fostering innovation through listening. For example, after the completion of a project, a leader might hold a debriefing session to gather input from team members about what worked well and what could be improved. This practice not only encourages continuous improvement but also reinforces the idea that team members play a crucial role in the organization's success.

Furthermore, leaders can leverage technology to enhance listening for innovation. Platforms that facilitate anonymous feedback or idea submissions can provide team members with a comfortable outlet to share their thoughts without the pressures of face-to-face interactions. This is especially beneficial for organizations with remote teams or those that have diverse employees who may feel hesitant to speak up in traditional settings. By harnessing the power of listening, leaders can

Listening

cultivate a culture where innovation thrives, leading to a more agile and forward-thinking organization.

3. Empathy

---

*"Empathy is about finding echoes of another
person in yourself." — Mohsin Hamid*

Empathy is a cornerstone of effective leadership, allowing
leaders to connect deeply with their team members and
understand their needs, emotions, and perspectives. It involves
not just recognizing what others feel but also responding to those
feelings in a meaningful way. This chapter will explore the
significance of empathy in leadership, its impact on team
dynamics, and practical ways leaders can cultivate this vital skill.

3.1 The Power of Empathy in Leadership

Empathy can transform the way leaders interact with their teams.
By genuinely understanding and appreciating the emotions and
experiences of others, leaders can create a work environment
that fosters trust and collaboration. This connection not only
enhances relationships but also boosts employee morale and
engagement. When team members feel understood, they are
more likely to communicate openly, share ideas, and collaborate
effectively, which ultimately contributes to a more cohesive and
productive work environment.

Research has shown that empathetic leaders can significantly
influence team performance. According to a study published in
the Journal of Business and Psychology, leaders who demonstrate
empathy can inspire higher levels of commitment among

employees, leading to improved job satisfaction and reduced turnover rates. Empathy helps leaders navigate conflicts with greater ease, as they can see situations from multiple perspectives and find common ground. This ability to empathize not only benefits individual relationships but also enhances overall team dynamics, resulting in a more harmonious and productive workplace.

Furthermore, empathy fosters a culture of inclusivity. When leaders actively practice empathy, they send a message that all voices are valued, regardless of differences in background, experience, or opinion. This inclusivity can lead to greater creativity and innovation, as diverse perspectives are acknowledged and integrated into the decision-making process.

3.2 Building Emotional Intelligence

To harness the power of empathy, leaders must develop their emotional intelligence (EI). EI encompasses the ability to recognize, understand, and manage one's own emotions while also being attuned to the emotions of others. Leaders with high emotional intelligence can better navigate complex interpersonal situations, making them more effective in their roles.

One approach to building emotional intelligence is through self-reflection. Leaders should regularly take time to assess their own emotional responses and consider how these feelings may affect their interactions with others. Journaling can be an effective tool for this, allowing leaders to track their emotions, reflect on specific situations, and identify patterns in their behaviour.

Another vital component of emotional intelligence is self-regulation, which involves managing one's emotional responses, especially in high-stress situations. Leaders can practice techniques such as mindfulness or deep breathing to maintain composure and respond thoughtfully rather than react impulsively. This ability to regulate emotions not only benefits leaders personally but also set a positive example for their team, promoting a more emotionally intelligent workplace culture.

Moreover, seeking feedback from peers and team members can be invaluable for leaders aiming to enhance their emotional intelligence. By asking for input on their communication styles and emotional responses, leaders can gain insights into how their behaviour is perceived and where they may need to improve. This commitment to self-improvement demonstrates vulnerability and a willingness to grow, further fostering a culture of empathy and trust within the team.

3.3   Empathy in Action

Implementing empathy in leadership requires intentional actions that demonstrate understanding and compassion towards team members. One practical way leaders can embody empathy is by actively engaging in conversations that prioritize emotional connection. This can be achieved through regular one-on-one meetings, where leaders can check in with their team members on both personal and professional levels. By asking open-ended questions about their well-being, challenges, and aspirations, leaders show genuine interest in their team members' lives, which fosters a deeper connection.

For example, a leader might say, "I noticed you seemed a bit stressed during our last team meeting. How are you managing your workload?" This approach not only opens the door for dialogue but also communicates to the team member that their feelings are valid and worthy of attention. Such conversations can reveal underlying issues that may affect performance and morale, allowing leaders to address these concerns proactively.

Additionally, leaders can demonstrate empathy by practicing active support during difficult times. Whether it's personal challenges, such as family issues or professional setbacks, being there for team members can significantly enhance their trust in leadership. Leaders can offer flexible work arrangements, additional resources, or simply a listening ear during challenging times. For instance, if a team member is dealing with a family emergency, a leader might suggest temporary workload adjustments to help them navigate their situation more effectively. This level of support not only helps the individual but also cultivates a sense of loyalty and commitment within the team.

Furthermore, celebrating individual and team successes is another way to express empathy. Recognizing achievements, both big and small, fosters a positive environment where team members feel valued. Leaders should take the time to acknowledge the hard work and dedication of their team, whether through verbal praise, written notes, or team-wide announcements. This recognition reinforces the idea that leaders are attentive to their team's contributions and emotions, ultimately strengthening the bond between leadership and team members.

3.4   Handling Difficult Conversations with Empathy

Navigating difficult conversations is an inevitable part of leadership, but handling them with empathy can turn potential conflicts into opportunities for growth and understanding. When leaders approach these conversations with empathy, they can minimize defensiveness and foster a more open dialogue. The key to successful difficult conversations lies in preparation, active listening, and a focus on solutions.

Preparation is essential when approaching sensitive topics. Leaders should gather relevant information and anticipate potential reactions from the other party. By understanding the issue at hand, leaders can approach the conversation with a clear sense of purpose and direction. This not only demonstrates professionalism but also shows respect for the individual's time and feelings.

During the conversation, it is crucial for leaders to practice active listening. This means allowing the other person to express their thoughts and emotions fully before responding. Leaders can use phrases like, "I hear what you're saying, and it sounds like you're feeling..." to validate the other person's feelings. This approach helps to diffuse tension and fosters a sense of understanding.

Moreover, leaders should maintain a solution-oriented mindset throughout the conversation. Rather than focusing solely on the problem, they should work collaboratively with the other person to explore possible solutions. For example, if a team member is struggling with their performance, instead of simply addressing the shortcomings, a leader can ask, "What can we do together to improve this situation?" This shift from problem identification to collaborative problem-solving encourages a more positive outcome and reinforces the notion that both parties are working toward a common goal.

Handling difficult conversations with empathy not only resolves issues but also strengthens relationships. When team members feel supported and understood, they are more likely to engage positively in future discussions, contributing to a healthier and more productive work environment.

3.5 Empathy and Diversity

Empathy plays a pivotal role in fostering diversity and inclusion within organizations. As leaders navigate increasingly diverse workforces, understanding and appreciating the unique experiences, backgrounds, and perspectives of team members becomes paramount. Empathy helps create an environment where all individuals feel valued and understood, regardless of their differences.

One way to cultivate empathy in diverse teams is through cultural competence. Leaders should strive to understand the cultural backgrounds of their team members, which includes recognizing cultural norms, values, and communication styles. This understanding not only enhances interpersonal relationships but also minimizes misunderstandings and conflicts that may arise from cultural differences. For example, a leader who is aware of the different cultural approaches to conflict resolution can facilitate discussions that respect these differences and promote effective problem-solving.

Additionally, actively encouraging open dialogue about diversity can foster an empathetic workplace culture. Leaders can create opportunities for team members to share their experiences, perspectives, and challenges related to diversity. This can be accomplished through facilitated discussions, diversity training sessions, or team-building exercises that highlight the value of different viewpoints. By encouraging team members to share their stories, leaders demonstrate their commitment to understanding the unique experiences of each individual, which strengthens bonds and promotes inclusivity.

Moreover, implementing mentorship programs can further enhance empathy within diverse teams. By pairing individuals from different backgrounds, organizations can foster cross-cultural understanding and create strong, supportive relationships. Mentorship not only empowers individuals but also encourages mentors to step into the shoes of their mentees, enhancing their empathy and understanding of diverse perspectives.

Empathy in leadership not only strengthens relationships but also drives innovation and creativity. When team members feel understood and valued, they are more likely to contribute their unique ideas and perspectives, leading to a more dynamic and successful organization. By prioritizing empathy, leaders can cultivate an inclusive environment that celebrates diversity, fosters collaboration, and ultimately drives organizational success.

4. Accountability

"The price of greatness is responsibility." –
Winston S. Churchill

Accountability is a fundamental aspect of effective leadership, representing a commitment to owning one's actions, decisions, and their outcomes. It involves not only taking responsibility for personal conduct but also fostering a culture where team members feel empowered to hold themselves and each other accountable. This chapter explores the significance of accountability in leadership, its role in creating a productive team environment, and practical strategies leaders can implement to promote accountability.

4.1 Leading by Example

A crucial element of accountability in leadership is the principle of leading by example. Leaders who model accountability demonstrate integrity and commitment to their values, setting a standard for their teams to follow. When leaders openly acknowledge their mistakes, learn from them, and take corrective action, they foster an environment where team members feel safe to do the same.

For instance, when a leader faces a setback on a project, they might share the experience with their team, discussing what went wrong and what could be improved. This transparency not only builds trust but also encourages a culture of learning rather than blame. Employees are more likely to embrace accountability when they see their leaders' admitting faults and striving for improvement.

Moreover, leading by example involves holding oneself accountable for the team's success as well. Leaders should ensure that their actions align with the team's goals and values. If a leader sets ambitious objectives, they must be diligent in their efforts to meet those expectations, showing that they are equally invested in the team's success.

4.2 Creating a Culture of Accountability

To establish a culture of accountability within an organization, leaders must implement systems and practices that support this principle. One effective approach is to set clear expectations for performance and behaviour. By articulating what is expected from each team member, leaders provide a framework for accountability that guides individual actions.

Regular performance reviews and feedback sessions are essential for maintaining accountability. These reviews should not only assess individual achievements but also focus on areas for growth. During these sessions, leaders can discuss any challenges faced by team members and work collaboratively to develop strategies for improvement. This ongoing dialogue reinforces the idea that accountability is a shared responsibility rather than a punitive measure.

Additionally, recognizing and celebrating accountability among team members can further reinforce this culture. When employees take ownership of their tasks and contribute positively to the team's objectives, leaders should acknowledge these efforts publicly. Celebrations of accountability not only motivate individuals but also inspire others to embrace the same commitment.

To promote accountability effectively, leaders should also establish consequences for failing to meet expectations. While it is essential to create a supportive environment, there must also be a recognition that actions have repercussions. By outlining consequences for non-compliance or lack of accountability, leaders reinforce the importance of this value within the organization.

4.3   Feedback Loops for Accountability

Establishing effective feedback loops is a vital strategy for promoting accountability within a team. Feedback loops facilitate ongoing communication between leaders and team members, ensuring that performance is continuously monitored and improved. These loops encourage a culture where accountability is not just a one-time discussion but an ongoing process.

Regular feedback sessions allow leaders to assess progress towards goals, discuss challenges, and provide guidance. These conversations should be structured to encourage two-way communication, where team members feel empowered to share their insights and experiences. For example, a leader might schedule monthly one-on-one meetings with each team member to review performance metrics and gather input on any obstacles they may be facing. This collaborative approach not only reinforces accountability but also demonstrates that leaders value their team's perspectives.

In addition to formal feedback sessions, leaders can leverage informal check-ins to foster accountability. Quick, casual conversations can provide an opportunity for team members to discuss their progress and address any immediate concerns. These informal interactions build rapport and reinforce a culture of accountability, as team members feel more comfortable discussing challenges without the pressure of a formal review.

Moreover, implementing 360-degree feedback can enhance accountability by incorporating input from multiple sources. This process allows team members to receive feedback from peers, supervisors, and even subordinates, providing a comprehensive view of their performance. This holistic approach to feedback can identify areas for improvement that may not be visible from a single perspective, fostering a deeper understanding of accountability within the team.

Finally, leaders should emphasize the importance of actionable feedback. Constructive feedback should focus on specific behaviours and outcomes, enabling team members to understand exactly what is expected of them. By providing clear and actionable suggestions for improvement, leaders empower team members to take ownership of their development and enhance their accountability.

4.4   Dealing with Mistakes and Failures

Mistakes and failures are inevitable in any organizational setting, and how leaders handle these situations can significantly impact team accountability and morale. Embracing a mindset that views mistakes as learning opportunities is essential for fostering an accountable culture. When leaders approach errors constructively, they encourage team members to take risks, innovate, and learn without the fear of punitive repercussions.

One effective strategy for dealing with mistakes is to conduct post-mortem analyses after significant failures or setbacks. This process involves gathering the team to discuss what went wrong, what could have been done differently, and how similar issues can be avoided in the future. During these discussions, it is crucial for leaders to create a safe space where team members feel comfortable sharing their thoughts and experiences. This openness fosters collective accountability, as everyone contributes to understanding and resolving the issue.

For example, if a project fails to meet its deadlines due to unforeseen challenges, a leader can initiate a post-mortem meeting to explore the factors that led to the failure. By encouraging team members to share their insights and perspectives, leaders can identify systemic issues that may have contributed to the setback. This collaborative approach not only helps the team learn from the experience but also reinforces the idea that accountability is a shared responsibility.

Additionally, leaders should emphasize the importance of taking responsibility for mistakes. When leaders openly admit their own errors, it sets a powerful example for team members. This vulnerability humanizes leadership and encourages employees to take ownership of their actions. For instance, a leader might share a personal story of a mistake they made early in their career and how it shaped their approach to accountability. Such narratives resonate with team members, fostering an environment where accountability is valued and embraced.

Furthermore, it's important for leaders to shift the focus from blame to solution-oriented thinking. Instead of assigning blame when something goes wrong, leaders should encourage discussions about how to fix the problem and prevent similar issues in the future. This proactive approach not only enhances accountability but also cultivates a culture of resilience, where team members feel empowered to learn and grow from their experiences.

4.5   Holding Others Accountable Respectfully

While accountability is essential for effective leadership, it must be balanced with respect and understanding. Holding others accountable does not mean criticizing or punishing them; rather, it involves guiding them towards improved performance in a supportive manner. Leaders can achieve this by maintaining open lines of communication and fostering a culture of trust.

When addressing performance issues, leaders should focus on constructive feedback rather than harsh criticism. For example, instead of saying, "You did not complete this task on time," a leader might say, "I noticed that the deadline was missed. Can we discuss what challenges you faced, and how we can ensure this doesn't happen in the future?" This approach encourages dialogue and demonstrates that the leader is invested in the employee's success.

Additionally, it is important for leaders to be consistent in holding team members accountable. Consistency builds trust and respect, as employees know what to expect from their leaders. If a leader holds one person accountable for a mistake but overlooks similar behaviour in another, it can lead to feelings of unfairness and resentment. By applying accountability standards uniformly, leaders foster a sense of equity within the team.

Moreover, leaders should also recognize and reward accountability when they see it. Acknowledging team members who take responsibility for their actions, learn from their mistakes, and actively seek improvement reinforces the value of accountability within the organization. By celebrating accountability, leaders not only encourage continued responsible behaviour but also contribute to a positive team culture.

Accountability

Ultimately, accountability is about creating a supportive environment where team members feel empowered to take ownership of their actions and decisions. By balancing accountability with respect and understanding, leaders can build a strong, resilient team committed to collective success.

5. Decisiveness

"In any moment of decision, the best thing you can do is the right thing. The next best thing is the wrong thing. The worst thing you can do is nothing." – Theodore Roosevelt

Decisiveness is a critical skill for leaders, encompassing the ability to make timely, informed decisions that drive organizational success. In a fast-paced business environment, leaders often face complex choices that can significantly impact their teams and overall objectives. This chapter explores the importance of decisiveness in leadership, the factors influencing effective decision-making, and strategies to enhance this essential skill.

5.1 The Cost of Indecision

Indecision can have detrimental effects on an organization, leading to missed opportunities, decreased morale, and wasted resources. When leaders hesitate to make decisions, it creates uncertainty within the team, undermining confidence and trust. Team members may feel anxious about the future and become disengaged when they perceive a lack of direction.

One notable example of the costs of indecision is seen in companies that fail to pivot quickly in response to market changes. For instance, during the early days of digital disruption, several retail giants hesitated to adopt e-commerce strategies, leading to significant losses and, in some cases, bankruptcy. In contrast, companies that embraced decisive leadership and quickly adapted to new market demands often gained a competitive advantage.

To mitigate the risks associated with indecision, leaders must recognize the importance of timely decision-making. A clear understanding of the potential consequences of both action and inaction can help leaders weigh their options effectively. Leaders should also encourage a culture that embraces experimentation, where taking calculated risks is seen as a necessary part of growth. By fostering an environment where decisions are made confidently and swiftly, organizations can position themselves for success.

5.2   Data-Driven Decision-Making

In today's data-rich environment, leveraging information to guide decisions is essential for effective leadership. Data-driven decision-making involves utilizing quantitative and qualitative data to inform choices, minimizing reliance on intuition alone. By integrating data into the decision-making process, leaders can make more informed, objective choices that are grounded in reality.

To implement data-driven decision-making, leaders must first identify key performance indicators (KPIs) relevant to their organization's goals. These KPIs serve as benchmarks for evaluating performance and understanding trends. For example, a sales leader might track metrics such as conversion rates, customer acquisition costs, and sales growth to inform decisions about marketing strategies and resource allocation.

Moreover, leaders should foster a culture of data literacy within their teams. This involves training team members to understand

and interpret data effectively, enabling them to contribute to the decision-making process. By empowering employees to analyze data and present their findings, leaders can enhance collective intelligence and ensure that decisions are well-informed.

It's also crucial for leaders to remain flexible and open to new information. As new data emerges, leaders must be willing to reassess their decisions and adapt their strategies accordingly. This agility not only enhances the quality of decisions but also demonstrates to the team that leadership is committed to continuous improvement and responsiveness.

Effective decision-making is a balancing act between intuition and data. While data provides valuable insights, leaders should also trust their instincts and experiences. Integrating both approaches allows for a more holistic view of the situation, leading to better outcomes.

5.3   Balancing Logic and Intuition

Effective decision-making often requires a delicate balance between logical analysis and intuitive judgment. Leaders must harness both cognitive reasoning and gut feelings to navigate complex situations. While data and analytical frameworks provide valuable insights, intuition can serve as a crucial complement, particularly in scenarios where time is limited or data is incomplete.

Logic involves the systematic evaluation of information and facts. Leaders should rely on critical thinking skills to assess available data, consider potential outcomes, and weigh pros and cons before making decisions. Tools such as SWOT analysis (Strengths, Weaknesses, Opportunities, Threats) can help leaders visualize their options and make informed choices. For instance, if a company is considering launching a new product, a leader might gather data on market trends, customer preferences, and competitive landscapes to evaluate the feasibility of the initiative.

Conversely, intuition stems from a leader's experiences and subconscious insights. It often plays a significant role in high-pressure situations where quick decisions are essential. For example, a seasoned executive might intuitively sense when to pivot a strategy based on a combination of market cues and past experiences, even if comprehensive data isn't immediately available. While intuition is subjective and can vary among individuals, it is often honed over time through exposure and learning.

To effectively balance logic and intuition, leaders can adopt a structured decision-making process that incorporates both elements. This approach may involve outlining a clear framework for analyzing data while allowing space for personal insights. Leaders should encourage team members to voice their intuitive thoughts during discussions, fostering an environment where both analytical and intuitive perspectives are valued.

Ultimately, the most effective leaders are those who can synthesize data-driven analysis with instinctual understanding, enabling them to make sound decisions that resonate with their teams and align with organizational goals.

5.4 Risk Assessment and Decision-Making

Understanding and managing risk is a crucial aspect of decisiveness in leadership. Every decision carries inherent risks, and leaders must be adept at identifying, evaluating, and mitigating these risks to make informed choices. A systematic approach to risk assessment can significantly enhance a leader's decision-making capabilities.

The first step in risk assessment is identifying potential risks associated with a decision. This involves considering various factors, such as financial implications, operational challenges, and market dynamics. For instance, when considering a major investment in new technology, leaders should analyze potential risks, including implementation costs, employee training needs, and market readiness.

Once risks are identified, leaders should evaluate the likelihood and impact of each risk. This assessment allows leaders to prioritize risks based on their potential effects on the organization. A risk matrix can be an effective tool for visualizing this assessment, categorizing risks into high, medium, and low levels based on their likelihood of occurrence and severity of impact.

Leaders must also develop mitigation strategies for significant risks. This may involve creating contingency plans, reallocating resources, or adjusting timelines to minimize exposure. For example, if a company is considering launching a new product in a volatile market, leaders might establish a phased rollout plan, allowing for adjustments based on initial customer feedback.

Furthermore, effective risk management requires a culture of open communication within the team. Encouraging team members to voice concerns and share insights can lead to a more comprehensive understanding of potential risks and enhance decision-making quality. By fostering a collaborative environment, leaders can harness diverse perspectives and experiences to identify risks that may not be immediately apparent.

By integrating risk assessment into the decision-making process, leaders can make more informed choices that not only consider immediate outcomes but also account for long-term implications.

This proactive approach fosters a culture of accountability and resilience within the organization.

5.5 Learning from Decisive Leaders

Studying the actions and strategies of successful leaders can provide valuable insights into effective decision-making. Decisive leaders often share common traits that contribute to their ability to make timely and impactful decisions. By analyzing their approaches, aspiring leaders can cultivate similar skills and mindsets.

One exemplary figure in decisiveness is Indra Nooyi, former CEO of PepsiCo. During her tenure, Nooyi faced numerous challenges, including shifting consumer preferences towards healthier options. Rather than hesitating, she made bold decisions to transform PepsiCo's product lineup. Nooyi championed the "Performance with Purpose" initiative, prioritizing nutrition and sustainability. Her willingness to embrace change, even at the risk of initial backlash, illustrates the power of decisive leadership in driving organizational evolution.

Another notable example is Satya Nadella, CEO of Microsoft, who took the helm in 2014. Nadella's decisive action to pivot Microsoft's focus toward cloud computing and artificial intelligence revitalized the company. He encouraged a culture of innovation and collaboration, enabling teams to make decisions quickly while aligning with a clear vision. Nadella's ability to assess the market landscape and act decisively on opportunities has positioned Microsoft as a leader in the tech industry.

Learning from these leaders involves understanding key aspects of their decision-making processes:

Decisiveness

1. Vision and Clarity: Successful leaders maintain a clear vision of their organization's goals. This clarity allows them to make decisions that align with long-term objectives, reducing ambiguity and enhancing focus.

2. Flexibility: Decisive leaders exhibit a willingness to adapt their strategies based on new information or changing circumstances. This flexibility enables them to respond to challenges effectively while remaining committed to their vision.

3. Empowerment: Great leaders empower their teams to make decisions within their areas of expertise. By delegating authority, they encourage accountability and promote a sense of ownership among team members, leading to more informed and timely decisions.

4. Learning Mindset: Decisive leaders understand that not all decisions will yield positive outcomes. They view setbacks as opportunities for learning and growth. This mindset fosters resilience and encourages teams to experiment and innovate without fear of failure.

By studying and emulating the decision-making strategies of effective leaders, aspiring leaders can develop their decisiveness and drive organizational success. The ability to act swiftly and confidently is a hallmark of strong leadership, contributing to both individual and collective achievements within an organization.

6. Empowerment

"The greatest gift of leadership is a boss who wants you to be successful." – Jon Taffer

E mpowerment is a fundamental aspect of effective leadership that fosters a sense of ownership and motivation among team members. When leaders empower their teams, they create an environment where individuals feel valued, supported, and capable of making meaningful contributions. This chapter delves into the principles of empowerment, its benefits, and practical strategies leaders can employ to inspire and enable their teams to excel.

6.1 What Empowerment Looks Like in Action

Empowerment manifests in various ways within an organization, leading to heightened engagement and productivity. It involves granting individuals the authority, resources, and support they need to take initiative and make decisions within their roles. Empowered employees are more likely to feel a sense of ownership over their work, leading to improved morale and motivation.

One of the hallmarks of empowerment is delegation. When leaders delegate responsibilities, they signal trust in their team's abilities and judgment. For instance, a marketing manager may empower a team member to lead a project, allowing them to make decisions on strategy and execution. This not only boosts the employee's confidence but also encourages them to develop leadership skills.

Additionally, empowerment can be reflected in open communication. Leaders who foster a culture of transparency and encourage feedback create an environment where team members feel comfortable sharing their ideas and opinions. Regular check-ins, brainstorming sessions, and collaborative decision-making processes can significantly enhance team dynamics and lead to innovative solutions.

Empowerment also involves recognizing and celebrating achievements. Leaders should acknowledge the contributions of their team members and provide positive reinforcement. This recognition can take various forms, such as public acknowledgment in team meetings or personalized notes of appreciation. By celebrating successes, leaders reinforce a sense of accomplishment and motivate their teams to strive for excellence.

Ultimately, empowerment is about enabling individuals to take ownership of their work and feel confident in their abilities. When employees are empowered, they become more engaged, productive, and invested in the success of the organization.

6.2 Delegating with Purpose

Delegation is a critical skill for leaders looking to empower their teams effectively. However, delegation is not merely about offloading tasks; it requires thoughtful consideration of how to distribute responsibilities in a way that maximizes impact and supports team development.

To delegate with purpose, leaders should first assess the strengths and capabilities of their team members. Understanding individual skills, interests, and areas for growth allows leaders to assign tasks that align with each person's expertise. For instance, if a team member has a background in data analysis, a leader may delegate responsibilities related to performance metrics or market research to leverage that expertise effectively.

Clear communication is also essential in the delegation process. Leaders should outline expectations, objectives, and deadlines while providing the necessary context for the task at hand. This clarity enables team members to understand the significance of their work and how it contributes to broader organizational goals. Additionally, leaders should ensure that team members have access to the resources and support needed to complete their tasks successfully.

Monitoring progress and providing constructive feedback are vital components of effective delegation. While leaders should give team members the autonomy to complete their tasks, they must also remain available for guidance and support. Regular check-ins can facilitate open dialogue and allow leaders to address any challenges team members may face. This approach not only reinforces trust but also fosters a collaborative atmosphere where individuals feel comfortable seeking help.

Ultimately, purposeful delegation empowers team members to take ownership of their responsibilities while enabling leaders to focus on higher-level strategic initiatives. By effectively distributing tasks, leaders can cultivate a sense of accountability and inspire their teams to reach their full potential.

6.3 Empowerment Through Trust

Trust is the cornerstone of effective empowerment in leadership. When leaders cultivate an environment of trust, they empower their teams to take initiative and make decisions without the fear of micromanagement or retribution. This sense of security allows team members to engage fully in their roles, fostering creativity and collaboration.

Building trust begins with transparency. Leaders must communicate openly about their expectations, goals, and decision-making processes. When team members understand the rationale behind a leader's decisions, they are more likely to feel included and valued. For example, during team meetings, leaders can share insights about organizational challenges and involve team members in discussions about potential solutions. This transparency not only builds trust but also encourages a collaborative approach to problem-solving.

Consistency is another vital element of trust. Leaders who consistently demonstrate integrity, fairness, and reliability foster a stable environment for their teams. When leaders follow through on commitments and treat team members with respect, they create a culture where individuals feel safe to express their opinions and take risks. Consistency in behaviour reinforces a leader's credibility and establishes a foundation for strong relationships.

Empowering teams through trust also involves granting autonomy. Leaders should resist the urge to micromanage and instead provide team members with the freedom to make decisions within their roles. This autonomy not only boosts confidence but also encourages individuals to develop critical thinking and problem-solving skills. For instance, allowing a project manager to make budgetary decisions can lead to innovative approaches and a deeper sense of ownership over the project's success.

Moreover, leaders must recognize that trust is built over time through shared experiences and mutual respect. By investing in team relationships and demonstrating genuine care for team members' well-being, leaders can create a trusting atmosphere where empowerment thrives. Team-building activities, mentorship programs, and opportunities for collaboration can further enhance trust among team members.

In conclusion, empowering through trust enables leaders to cultivate high-performing teams that are resilient, innovative, and committed to organizational success. By fostering a culture of trust, leaders can inspire their teams to take initiative, embrace challenges, and contribute to a shared vision.

6.4 Removing Obstacles for Your Team

To truly empower their teams, leaders must actively identify and remove obstacles that hinder progress. These barriers can take many forms, including organizational inefficiencies, communication breakdowns, and lack of resources. By addressing these challenges, leaders can create an environment that fosters empowerment and enables team members to excel.

One of the primary obstacles to empowerment is bureaucracy. Complex organizational structures and cumbersome processes can stifle creativity and slow down decision-making. Leaders should evaluate existing workflows and identify areas where they can streamline operations. For example, implementing agile methodologies can help teams respond more quickly to changing needs and reduce unnecessary red tape. By creating a more agile environment, leaders empower their teams to act swiftly and confidently.

Communication barriers can also impede empowerment. Leaders must encourage open lines of communication across all levels of the organization. This involves not only promoting transparency but also actively soliciting feedback from team members. Regular check-ins, anonymous surveys, and open-door policies can facilitate communication and help leaders identify potential obstacles early on. When team members feel heard and valued, they are more likely to contribute ideas and solutions.

Additionally, resource allocation is critical for empowering teams. Leaders should ensure that their teams have access to the tools, training, and support needed to succeed. This may involve investing in professional development opportunities, providing mentorship programs, or equipping teams with the latest technology. For example, if a sales team struggles due to outdated software, investing in modern CRM tools can enhance their efficiency and effectiveness.

Furthermore, leaders should be proactive in addressing any interpersonal conflicts that may arise within teams. Conflict can hinder collaboration and reduce morale. By fostering a culture of open dialogue and conflict resolution, leaders can empower team members to address issues constructively. Providing conflict resolution training and facilitating mediation sessions can equip teams with the skills needed to navigate disagreements.

In summary, removing obstacles for your team is essential for fostering a culture of empowerment. By streamlining processes, enhancing communication, ensuring access to resources, and addressing conflicts, leaders create an environment where team members can thrive and contribute meaningfully to organizational goals.

6.5   Recognition and Empowerment

Recognition plays a crucial role in empowerment, reinforcing the value of individual contributions and fostering a sense of belonging within a team. When leaders acknowledge the efforts and achievements of their team members, they not only motivate individuals but also strengthen the overall team dynamic. Empowerment through recognition creates an environment where employees feel valued and inspired to excel.

One effective approach to recognition is through celebrating successes—both big and small. This can take various forms, such as public acknowledgments during team meetings, shout-outs in company newsletters, or even simple thank-you notes. Celebrating milestones, such as completing a project or achieving quarterly targets, provides an opportunity for leaders to express gratitude and highlight the contributions of team members. This recognition not only boosts morale but also reinforces a culture of appreciation and teamwork.

Another powerful method is creating recognition programs that align with the values of the organization. Implementing awards, such as "Employee of the Month" or peer-nominated accolades, encourages team members to recognize each other's efforts. These programs can motivate employees to go above and beyond in their roles, fostering a collaborative environment where everyone feels empowered to contribute.

Leaders should also be mindful of the impact of individualized recognition. Understanding what motivates each team member can help tailor recognition efforts effectively. For example, while some individuals may appreciate public recognition, others may prefer a private acknowledgment. Taking the time to understand these preferences allows leaders to empower their team members in a way that resonates personally. Regular one-on-one meetings provide an opportunity to check in on team members, offering leaders insights into how they can best support and recognize each individual.

Moreover, integrating recognition into the organizational culture ensures that it becomes a consistent practice rather than an occasional event. Leaders can encourage team members to recognize each other regularly, creating a supportive environment where everyone feels empowered to celebrate collective achievements. This approach fosters camaraderie and strengthens the bonds within the team, leading to increased collaboration and innovation.

In summary, recognition is a vital aspect of empowerment in leadership. By celebrating successes, creating recognition programs, personalizing acknowledgments, and fostering a culture of appreciation, leaders can enhance motivation and engagement within their teams. When team members feel recognized and valued, they are more likely to take ownership of their work and contribute meaningfully to the organization's success.

7. Resilience

> *"It's not whether you get knocked down; it's whether you get up." – Vince Lombardi*

Resilience is an essential quality for leaders, enabling them to navigate challenges, adapt to change, and inspire their teams to persevere in the face of adversity. In a rapidly evolving world, resilience fosters a culture of strength, determination, and adaptability, empowering leaders and their teams to bounce back from setbacks and emerge stronger than before. This chapter explores the principles of resilience, effective strategies to cultivate it within individuals and teams, and the importance of fostering a resilient mindset in leadership.

7.1 Developing a Resilient Mindset

A resilient mindset is characterized by the ability to view challenges as opportunities for growth rather than insurmountable obstacles. Developing such a mindset begins with self-awareness—recognizing one's emotions, reactions, and thought patterns in the face of adversity. Leaders must take the time to reflect on their responses to setbacks, understanding that resilience is not about avoiding difficulties but rather embracing them as part of the journey.

One key aspect of building resilience is fostering a sense of optimism. Resilient individuals tend to have a positive outlook, believing that they can overcome challenges and learn from experiences. Leaders can cultivate optimism by reframing negative thoughts and focusing on solutions rather than problems. For example, instead of dwelling on a failed project, a leader might encourage the team to analyze what went wrong, identify lessons learned, and brainstorm ideas for improvement moving forward. This proactive approach not only builds resilience but also encourages a growth mindset among team members.

Emotional regulation is another critical component of resilience. Leaders should develop strategies to manage stress, anxiety, and frustration during challenging times. Mindfulness practices, such as meditation or deep-breathing exercises, can help leaders stay grounded and focused, enabling them to respond thoughtfully rather than react impulsively. Encouraging team members to engage in similar practices fosters a collective sense of calm and resilience within the team.

Additionally, fostering a strong support network is essential for building resilience. Leaders should create an environment where team members feel comfortable seeking help and support from one another. This can involve establishing mentorship programs, team-building activities, and regular check-ins to foster open communication and collaboration. When individuals know they can rely on their colleagues for support, they are more likely to face challenges with confidence and resilience.

In summary, developing a resilient mindset involves cultivating self-awareness, optimism, emotional regulation, and a strong support network. Leaders who model these qualities empower their teams to embrace challenges, learn from setbacks, and emerge stronger in the face of adversity.

7.2   Leading Through Crisis

In times of crisis, effective leadership is crucial for guiding teams through uncertainty and turmoil. Leaders must be able to respond swiftly and decisively while instilling confidence and resilience within their teams. Leading through crisis requires a combination of strategic thinking, emotional intelligence, and clear communication.

First and foremost, leaders must assess the situation and gather relevant information to make informed decisions. This involves analyzing the crisis's impact on the organization and understanding the concerns and emotions of team members. Leaders should approach the situation with a calm and collected demeanor, as their reactions set the tone for how the team will respond. For instance, during a financial downturn, a leader might hold a meeting to discuss the challenges ahead while providing transparent updates on the organization's status and plans for recovery.

Effective communication is paramount during a crisis. Leaders must communicate clearly and regularly with their teams, providing updates, guidance, and reassurance. Transparency fosters trust and helps alleviate anxiety among team members. Acknowledging the difficulties while also emphasizing the organization's strengths and potential for recovery is essential. Leaders should encourage open dialogue, allowing team members to voice their concerns and ask questions. This open line of communication helps create a sense of unity and shared purpose during challenging times.

Furthermore, leaders must demonstrate flexibility and adaptability in their approach. Crises often require leaders to pivot quickly, adjusting strategies and priorities as new information emerges. Being open to feedback and willing to adapt plans based on evolving circumstances empowers teams to feel involved and valued in the decision-making process.

Ultimately, leading through a crisis involves being a source of strength and stability for the team. By remaining composed, communicating effectively, and demonstrating adaptability, leaders can inspire resilience and motivate their teams to overcome challenges together.

7.3 Learning from Failures and Setbacks

Learning from failures and setbacks is a vital aspect of building resilience in leadership. In the face of adversity, leaders must shift their perspective from viewing failure as a negative outcome to embracing it as an opportunity for growth and development. This approach not only fosters resilience but also sets a powerful example for team members, encouraging them to view challenges through a lens of opportunity.

First, it is essential for leaders to analyze failures objectively. This involves conducting a thorough assessment of what went wrong, identifying the contributing factors, and determining how similar mistakes can be avoided in the future. Rather than assigning blame, leaders should create a culture where team members feel safe to discuss failures openly. For instance, conducting post-mortem meetings after project setbacks allows teams to share insights and lessons learned in a constructive manner. By focusing on the "what" and "how" rather than the "who," leaders can foster a culture of accountability and continuous improvement.

Moreover, encouraging a growth mindset is crucial in the learning process. A growth mindset—the belief that abilities and intelligence can be developed through dedication and hard work—empowers individuals to embrace challenges and persist despite setbacks. Leaders should reinforce this mindset by praising effort and resilience rather than just outcomes. For example, recognizing a team member's perseverance in tackling a difficult project, even if the project did not meet its initial goals, sends a powerful message that resilience is valued.

Additionally, leaders should actively share their own experiences of failure and learning with their teams. When leaders are transparent about their setbacks and the lessons they learned, it humanizes them and fosters a deeper connection with team members. This openness creates a safe space for employees to share their own experiences without fear of judgment. By cultivating an environment where learning from failures is normalized, leaders empower their teams to take risks and innovate.

Finally, leaders must reinforce the concept that failure is not the end but rather a step in the journey towards success. Highlighting stories of successful individuals who experienced significant failures before achieving their goals can be inspirational. For instance, leaders can share the journey of renowned figures like Thomas Edison, who famously said, "I have not failed. I've just found 10,000 ways that won't work." These narratives remind teams that setbacks are a natural part of the learning process and that perseverance is key to eventual success.

In summary, learning from failures and setbacks is fundamental to developing resilience in leadership. By analyzing failures, encouraging a growth mindset, sharing personal experiences, and reframing failures as opportunities, leaders can empower their teams to embrace challenges and emerge stronger from adversity.

7.4   Building a Resilient Team

A resilient team is one that can navigate challenges effectively, adapt to change, and support one another through adversity. As leaders work to foster resilience within their teams, they must focus on creating a supportive environment that encourages collaboration, communication, and shared responsibility. Building a resilient team involves implementing several key strategies that empower individuals to thrive in the face of challenges.

First and foremost, leaders should promote collaboration and teamwork. Resilient teams thrive when members work together towards common goals, leveraging each other's strengths and supporting one another during difficult times. Leaders can facilitate collaboration by creating opportunities for team-building activities and encouraging cross-functional projects. These initiatives help build trust and camaraderie, enabling team members to rely on each other for support during challenging situations.

Effective communication is another critical component of building a resilient team. Leaders should foster an environment where team members feel comfortable sharing their thoughts, concerns, and ideas. Regular team meetings, open forums for discussion, and feedback sessions can enhance communication and ensure that everyone feels heard. By promoting transparency and openness, leaders empower their teams to address challenges collectively, leading to more innovative solutions.

Additionally, leaders should focus on developing the skills and competencies of their team members. Providing training opportunities, mentorship programs, and resources for professional development equips individuals with the tools they need to adapt to change and overcome obstacles. When team members feel competent and capable, they are more likely to approach challenges with confidence and resilience.

Furthermore, fostering a culture of celebration and recognition is essential in building resilience. Acknowledging individual and team achievements reinforces a sense of accomplishment and motivation. Regularly celebrating milestones and successes, even in small ways, helps maintain morale and reminds team members of their collective strength. Leaders can create recognition programs that highlight team efforts, encouraging individuals to take pride in their contributions.

In conclusion, building a resilient team requires a multifaceted approach that emphasizes collaboration, communication, skill development, and recognition. By cultivating an environment where team members support one another and feel empowered to face challenges, leaders can create a resilient team that is capable of overcoming adversity and achieving collective success.

7.5   Personal Well-being and Resilience

Personal well-being is a foundational pillar of resilience in leadership. Leaders who prioritize their physical, mental, and emotional health are better equipped to handle the stresses and challenges that come with their roles. The interplay between personal well-being and resilience is profound, as a leader's state of well-being directly impacts their ability to inspire and guide their teams through adversity.

To cultivate personal well-being, leaders should first focus on self-care practices. This can include regular physical exercise, maintaining a balanced diet, ensuring adequate sleep, and engaging in activities that bring joy and relaxation. Physical well-being significantly contributes to mental clarity and emotional stability. Leaders who model self-care not only enhance their own resilience but also encourage team members to prioritize their well-being. For instance, a leader who incorporates wellness breaks or flexible working hours can foster a culture that values health and balance.

Moreover, mindfulness and stress management techniques are essential for maintaining personal well-being. Mindfulness practices, such as meditation, deep-breathing exercises, and yoga, can help leaders manage stress and improve emotional regulation. These practices allow leaders to remain present, focused, and centred, even in turbulent times. By integrating mindfulness into their routines, leaders can enhance their ability to respond thoughtfully to challenges rather than react impulsively.

Creating a supportive network is another vital aspect of personal well-being. Leaders should cultivate relationships with mentors, peers, and coaches who can provide guidance, support, and perspective. Sharing experiences and challenges with others can alleviate feelings of isolation and help leaders gain valuable insights into their situations. By engaging in networking and professional development opportunities, leaders can also foster a sense of community, reinforcing the importance of collaboration and support in overcoming adversity.

Furthermore, leaders must embrace work-life balance as a core principle of their leadership approach. The demands of leadership can often blur the lines between personal and professional life, leading to burnout and decreased resilience. Leaders should set boundaries around work hours, encourage their teams to do the same, and prioritize time for personal interests and family. By demonstrating a commitment to work-life balance, leaders not only protect their own well-being but also promote a culture that respects personal time and encourages employees to recharge.

Resilience

In summary, personal well-being is integral to building resilience in leadership. By prioritizing self-care, practicing mindfulness, cultivating supportive networks, and maintaining work-life balance, leaders can enhance their ability to face challenges with strength and adaptability. A leader who embodies well-being fosters a resilient team, inspiring individuals to thrive amidst adversity.

8.   Strategy

"A good strategy is like a compass. It keeps you headed in the right direction, even in turbulent times."

Strategy is essential in today's fast-paced and ever-changing business environment, developing and communicating a clear vision through effective for leaders. Strategy serves as the roadmap for organizational success, guiding decisions and actions while aligning teams with shared objectives. This chapter explores the significance of strategy in leadership, focusing on the development of a strategic vision, goal alignment, effective communication, adaptability to change, and the tools for strategic planning.

8.1   The Importance of a Strategic Vision

A strategic vision defines the future direction of an organization, articulating its long-term goals and aspirations. It serves as a beacon, guiding leaders and teams toward a common destination. A well-crafted vision not only provides clarity but also inspires and motivates employees to strive for a shared purpose.

To establish a powerful strategic vision, leaders must first engage in thorough market analysis and internal assessments. Understanding market trends, customer needs, and the competitive landscape is crucial. By analyzing strengths, weaknesses, opportunities, and threats (SWOT), leaders can identify areas where their organization can excel and define a vision that leverages these insights.

A strategic vision should also reflect the organization's core values and culture. Leaders must ensure that the vision aligns with the fundamental principles that guide their organization. For instance, if innovation is a core value, the vision should emphasize growth through creative solutions. By incorporating core values into the strategic vision, leaders can foster a sense of ownership and commitment among team members.

Moreover, leaders should involve key stakeholders in the visioning process. Collaborating with team members, customers, and partners allows for diverse perspectives, leading to a more comprehensive and inclusive vision. Engaging employees in shaping the vision fosters a sense of belonging and accountability, as they feel their voices are heard and valued.

In summary, the importance of a strategic vision lies in its ability to provide direction, inspire action, and align teams toward common goals. By conducting thorough analyses, incorporating core values, and involving stakeholders, leaders can develop a vision that drives organizational success.

8.2 Aligning Goals with Vision

Once a strategic vision is established, aligning organizational goals with that vision is critical. This alignment ensures that all efforts and resources are directed toward achieving the shared objectives. Leaders must create a clear connection between the vision and specific, measurable goals that guide daily operations.

The first step in aligning goals with vision is to set SMART goals— Specific, Measurable, Achievable, Relevant, and Time-bound. These criteria provide a structured framework for developing goals that are clear and actionable. For example, if the vision emphasizes customer satisfaction, a SMART goal might be to increase customer retention by 15% within the next year. Such specificity ensures that all team members understand what is expected and can work collaboratively toward the same targets.

Next, leaders should communicate the alignment between the goals and the strategic vision. This involves consistently reinforcing the message that each goal contributes to the larger vision. Regular team meetings, internal communications, and visual reminders, such as goal charts, can help keep this connection top of mind for all team members.

In addition to setting SMART goals, leaders should encourage cross-departmental collaboration. When different teams understand how their specific objectives contribute to the overarching vision, they can work together more effectively. For instance, marketing, sales, and customer service departments can align their efforts to enhance customer satisfaction, ensuring that all functions are working cohesively toward the same outcome.

Furthermore, leaders should conduct regular progress reviews to assess alignment. By monitoring the achievement of goals and evaluating their contribution to the vision, leaders can make informed adjustments as needed. This process fosters accountability and encourages teams to reflect on their performance continuously.

In summary, aligning organizational goals with the strategic vision is essential for success. By setting SMART goals, effectively communicating their connection to the vision, promoting collaboration, and conducting regular reviews, leaders can ensure that all efforts contribute to achieving the desired future state.

8.3 Communicating Vision Effectively

Effective communication of the strategic vision is critical to ensure that all members of an organization understand and embrace the direction in which they are heading. When leaders articulate their vision clearly and compellingly, they foster a sense of purpose and alignment among their teams, enabling everyone to work together toward shared goals.

First and foremost, clarity is essential. Leaders should avoid jargon and complex language that may confuse team members. Instead, they should communicate the vision in simple, relatable terms that resonate with employees at all levels. A well-crafted vision statement should be concise and memorable, making it easy for employees to recall and reference in their daily work. For example, using relatable metaphors or analogies can help illustrate complex concepts and make the vision more tangible.

Moreover, leaders should utilize various communication channels to reach their audience effectively. In today's digital age, relying solely on one method of communication, such as email, is insufficient. Instead, leaders should employ a multi-channel approach that includes team meetings, town halls, internal newsletters, and digital platforms. Utilizing visuals, such as infographics or videos, can also enhance understanding and engagement. For instance, a video presentation of the strategic vision can create an emotional connection and reinforce its importance.

Engaging employees in two-way communication is equally vital. Leaders should encourage questions, feedback, and discussions around the vision. Creating forums for open dialogue, such as Q&A sessions or focus groups, allows team members to express their thoughts and concerns, fostering a sense of ownership in the vision. This participatory approach not only strengthens commitment but also helps leaders gain valuable insights that can refine the vision further.

Additionally, leaders should ensure that the vision is consistently reinforced in daily operations. Regularly referencing the vision in meetings, performance reviews, and company communications can keep it at the forefront of employees' minds. Celebrating milestones that align with the vision serves as a reminder of the collective journey and reinforces its significance.

Finally, leaders should embrace storytelling as a powerful tool for communicating the vision. Sharing stories about how the vision has impacted individuals, teams, or customers can make it relatable and inspiring. Personal anecdotes or case studies can illustrate the vision's practical implications and motivate employees to embrace it wholeheartedly. For instance, a leader might share a story about a team that achieved a breakthrough by embodying the strategic vision, highlighting the positive outcomes of aligning with it.

In conclusion, effectively communicating the strategic vision is essential for organizational alignment and success. By prioritizing clarity, utilizing various channels, encouraging two-way communication, reinforcing the vision in daily operations, and leveraging storytelling, leaders can inspire and engage their teams in working toward a shared future.

8.4   Adapting Strategy to Change

In an ever-evolving landscape, the ability to adapt strategy to change is a hallmark of effective leadership. As external factors such as market dynamics, technological advancements, and societal shifts impact organizations, leaders must remain agile and responsive. Adapting strategy involves not only recognizing when change is necessary but also implementing shifts that align with the organization's vision and goals.

The first step in adapting strategy is conducting regular environmental scans. Leaders should stay informed about industry trends, competitor activities, and changes in customer preferences. This proactive approach allows leaders to identify potential disruptions or opportunities before they become critical issues. Utilizing data analytics and market research can provide valuable insights that inform strategic adjustments.

Once a need for change is identified, leaders must engage in collaborative decision-making. Involving key stakeholders, including team members and subject matter experts, fosters a sense of ownership and inclusivity. By gathering diverse perspectives, leaders can make more informed decisions that consider various viewpoints and potential implications. This collaborative approach also helps build trust among team members, as they feel their insights are valued and integrated into the decision-making process.

Furthermore, leaders should embrace a culture of experimentation. Encouraging teams to test new ideas and approaches fosters innovation and agility. This involves creating an environment where calculated risks are accepted, and failure is viewed as an opportunity for learning rather than a setback. For instance, a leader might implement pilot programs to test new initiatives before fully committing to them, allowing for adjustments based on feedback and outcomes.

In addition to experimentation, leaders should prioritize effective change management. Implementing strategic changes requires careful planning and communication. Leaders must articulate the reasons for the change, its expected benefits, and the steps involved in the transition. Providing support and resources for team members during this process is crucial to minimize resistance and facilitate smooth adaptation. Training programs, workshops, and ongoing support can help equip employees with the skills and knowledge needed to navigate the changes effectively.

Finally, leaders should regularly evaluate and adjust strategies as needed. Monitoring the outcomes of implemented changes is essential to ensure they align with the organization's vision and goals. By establishing key performance indicators (KPIs) and regularly reviewing progress, leaders can make data-driven decisions about necessary adjustments. This ongoing evaluation process reinforces a culture of continuous improvement and adaptability.

In summary, adapting strategy to change is essential for effective leadership in today's dynamic environment. By conducting environmental scans, engaging in collaborative decision-making, fostering a culture of experimentation, prioritizing change management, and regularly evaluating outcomes, leaders can navigate change successfully and guide their organizations toward sustained success.

8.5 Tools for Strategic Planning

Strategic planning is essential for translating a visionary strategy into actionable steps that guide an organization toward its goals. Various tools and methodologies can aid leaders in the strategic planning process, ensuring that their strategies are well-structured and adaptable to changing circumstances. This section will explore some of the most effective tools for strategic planning, helping leaders navigate complexities and enhance decision-making.

One of the foundational tools in strategic planning is the SWOT analysis. This framework allows leaders to evaluate the organization's Strengths, Weaknesses, Opportunities, and Threats. By conducting a thorough SWOT analysis, leaders can identify internal capabilities and limitations while also exploring external factors that could impact their strategy. For example, a technology company may recognize its strengths in innovation and skilled workforce but also acknowledge weaknesses in market reach and brand recognition. By identifying opportunities, such as emerging markets or technological advancements, and potential threats, like increased competition, leaders can make informed decisions about strategic directions and resource allocation.

Another valuable tool is the PESTLE analysis, which examines the Political, Economic, Social, Technological, Legal, and Environmental factors that influence an organization. This analysis provides a comprehensive view of the external environment, helping leaders understand the broader context in which they operate. For instance, understanding political factors such as government regulations or economic trends can aid leaders in anticipating changes that may affect their strategic initiatives. By conducting a PESTLE analysis, leaders can align their strategies with the external landscape, ensuring that their plans are resilient to potential disruptions.

In addition to these analyses, the use of strategic frameworks can provide structure to the planning process. Popular frameworks like the Balanced Scorecard or the Business Model Canvas can help leaders visualize their strategies and monitor progress. The Balanced Scorecard, for example, translates an organization's vision and strategy into a set of performance metrics across four perspectives: Financial, Customer, Internal Processes, and Learning & Growth. This holistic approach enables leaders to evaluate their strategy's effectiveness and adjust as needed, fostering a culture of accountability and continuous improvement.

Moreover, employing scenario planning can enhance strategic resilience. This method involves creating and analyzing different future scenarios based on various uncertainties. By envisioning multiple possible futures, leaders can prepare their organizations for different contingencies, ensuring that they can respond effectively to unexpected challenges. For instance, a company may develop scenarios based on economic fluctuations or shifts in consumer behaviour, allowing them to adapt their strategies proactively.

Lastly, incorporating data analytics and performance measurement tools is essential for monitoring the effectiveness of strategic initiatives. Leaders should leverage technology and analytics to track key performance indicators (KPIs) that align with their strategic goals. Regularly reviewing performance data enables leaders to assess progress, identify areas for improvement, and make informed adjustments to their strategies. Tools such as dashboards and reporting software can streamline this process, providing real-time insights into organizational performance.

In summary, leveraging various tools for strategic planning enhances leaders' ability to navigate complexities and drive organizational success. By utilizing SWOT and PESTLE analyses, strategic frameworks, scenario planning, and data analytics, leaders can develop well-informed strategies that are adaptable to changing circumstances. These tools empower leaders to translate their vision into actionable plans, fostering a culture of strategic thinking and continuous improvement.

9. Humility

> *"Humility is not thinking less of yourself, but thinking of yourself less."* — *C.S. Lewis*

Humility stands out as a vital quality for effective leadership. Humility in leadership fosters an environment of collaboration, openness, and trust, allowing teams to thrive and innovate. It encourages leaders to prioritize the needs and contributions of their team members while recognizing their own limitations and areas for growth. This chapter delves into the critical aspects of humility in leadership and how it contributes to lasting success.

9.1 The Role of Humility in Leadership

Humility is essential for effective leadership as it creates a culture of respect and collaboration within organizations. When leaders practice humility, they demonstrate that they value the contributions and perspectives of their team members. This openness fosters an environment where employees feel empowered to share their ideas, take risks, and provide constructive feedback without fear of reprisal. In such a culture, collaboration becomes the norm, leading to increased creativity and innovation.

Moreover, humble leaders are more approachable. They exhibit a willingness to listen and engage with their team, which helps build strong relationships. This approachability fosters trust, as employees feel that their opinions are respected and considered.

For example, when leaders actively seek input from their team on critical decisions, they show that they value diverse perspectives, further reinforcing a sense of inclusivity.

Humility also allows leaders to embrace vulnerability. By acknowledging their limitations and mistakes, humble leaders create an environment where learning from failures is encouraged. This vulnerability not only humanizes leaders but also inspires others to be open about their challenges, ultimately promoting a growth mindset throughout the organization. A leader who shares a story of overcoming a failure demonstrates resilience and encourages their team to persevere through difficulties.

Furthermore, humility encourages leaders to adopt a servant leadership mindset. This approach prioritizes the well-being of team members, focusing on their growth and success rather than merely pursuing personal ambitions. By serving their teams, humble leaders cultivate loyalty and commitment, as employees feel supported and valued. This shift in focus ultimately enhances team performance and satisfaction, leading to higher retention rates and productivity.

In summary, humility plays a crucial role in effective leadership. By fostering a culture of respect, approachability, vulnerability, and servant leadership, humble leaders create an environment where teams can thrive, driving organizational success.

9.2 Embracing Mistakes and Learning from Them

A critical aspect of humility in leadership is the ability to embrace mistakes and view them as opportunities for learning. Leaders who can acknowledge their missteps without defensiveness or denial create a culture that encourages experimentation and innovation. This section will explore the importance of embracing mistakes and the strategies leaders can employ to foster a learning-oriented environment.

First, leaders must recognize that mistakes are an inevitable part of growth. In a rapidly changing world, even the most seasoned leaders will encounter challenges and setbacks. Instead of hiding from these mistakes or blaming others, humble leaders take responsibility and view errors as valuable learning experiences. This mindset not only helps leaders grow personally but also encourages their teams to adopt a similar perspective.

When leaders openly share their experiences with mistakes, they normalize the concept of learning from failure. For instance, a leader who discusses a project that did not meet expectations can provide insights into what went wrong and the lessons learned. This transparency fosters a safe environment where team members feel comfortable sharing their mistakes and learning from them. By establishing this culture, leaders promote continuous improvement and innovation.

In addition to sharing personal experiences, leaders can implement processes that facilitate learning from mistakes. For example, conducting post-mortem analyses after projects allows teams to reflect on what worked, what didn't, and how they can improve in the future. By systematically evaluating outcomes, organizations can extract valuable insights and develop best practices, turning failures into stepping stones for success.

Furthermore, celebrating the lessons learned from mistakes can reinforce a learning culture. Leaders should acknowledge team members who demonstrate resilience and adaptability in the face of challenges. By highlighting these behaviours, leaders encourage others to take calculated risks and learn from their experiences, knowing that their efforts will be recognized and valued.

In summary, embracing mistakes and fostering a learning-oriented environment are vital components of humility in leadership. By taking responsibility, sharing experiences, implementing reflective processes, and celebrating learning moments, leaders can cultivate a culture of continuous improvement that drives innovation and success.

9.3 Balancing Confidence with Humility

While humility is a crucial trait for effective leadership, it is equally important to strike a balance between humility and confidence. Leaders must exude confidence to inspire their teams and navigate challenges effectively, but this confidence should not overshadow the essential quality of humility. This section explores how leaders can maintain this delicate balance to create an environment that fosters both respect and achievement.

Confidence in leadership is essential because it instils trust and assurance within a team. When leaders communicate their vision with conviction and decisiveness, it motivates employees to align their efforts with organizational goals. For instance, a confident leader who articulates a clear strategy can galvanize the team around shared objectives, fostering a sense of purpose and direction. However, confidence must be tempered with humility to prevent arrogance, which can alienate team members and stifle collaboration.

One-way leaders can balance confidence and humility is by practicing self-awareness. This involves recognizing one's strengths and limitations, understanding how one's behaviour affects others, and being open to feedback. Leaders who exhibit self-awareness demonstrate that they value the insights and contributions of their team members. For example, a leader might confidently present a new initiative but also invite feedback from team members, acknowledging that their perspectives can enhance the plan. This practice fosters a culture of open dialogue and collaboration, reinforcing the idea that leadership is a collective effort.

Additionally, leaders can practice servant leadership as a framework to maintain this balance. Servant leaders prioritize the needs of their team above their own, demonstrating that they are not only confident in their abilities but also committed to the growth and well-being of others. By empowering their teams and facilitating their development, these leaders cultivate a sense of shared responsibility and trust. For instance, a leader who delegates authority and supports team members in decision-making showcases confidence in their abilities while embodying humility by acknowledging that others can contribute valuable insights.

Moreover, leaders should encourage a growth mindset within their organizations. By fostering an environment where learning and development are prioritized, leaders demonstrate confidence in their team's potential while remaining humble in acknowledging that everyone, including themselves, can grow and improve. This approach can involve offering opportunities for training, mentorship, and collaborative projects that allow team members to showcase their talents. When leaders invest in their teams' growth, they reinforce the notion that success is a shared achievement rather than a solitary pursuit.

In summary, balancing confidence with humility is vital for effective leadership. By practicing self-awareness, embracing servant leadership, and fostering a growth mindset, leaders can create an environment that inspires trust and collaboration. This balance enables leaders to guide their teams toward success while remaining grounded and approachable, ultimately enhancing organizational performance.

9.4   Inviting Feedback and Critique

One of the most powerful practices a humble leader can adopt is the intentional invitation of feedback and critique from team members. This approach not only enhances the leader's self-awareness but also fosters a culture of continuous improvement within the organization. By demonstrating a willingness to receive input and engage in constructive dialogue, leaders can build trust and encourage open communication among their teams.

Inviting feedback begins with creating a safe environment where team members feel comfortable expressing their thoughts and opinions. Leaders must actively communicate that their team's insights are valued and that feedback is an essential component of growth. For example, a leader might hold regular feedback sessions where team members are encouraged to share their views on leadership decisions, project outcomes, or team dynamics. This practice not only promotes transparency but also empowers employees, making them feel that their voices matter.

Moreover, leaders should model the behaviour they wish to see in their teams. By actively seeking feedback on their own performance, leaders demonstrate humility and openness to improvement. This could involve asking specific questions such as, "What could I have done differently to support the team during this project?" or "Are there areas where I can improve my communication?" Such inquiries signal to team members that it is acceptable and encouraged to offer constructive criticism, thus fostering a culture of growth and development.

In addition to creating a safe space for feedback, leaders should ensure that they respond thoughtfully to the input they receive. It's crucial not just to listen but also to act on the feedback when appropriate. When leaders acknowledge feedback and demonstrate changes based on that input, they reinforce the value of team members' contributions. For instance, if a leader receives feedback about communication issues during a project, addressing those concerns in future meetings shows that the feedback was taken seriously. This responsiveness strengthens relationships and encourages ongoing dialogue.

Furthermore, leaders should embrace feedback from diverse sources. This means not only seeking input from direct reports but also welcoming perspectives from peers, mentors, and even customers. By broadening the scope of feedback, leaders can gain a more comprehensive understanding of their impact and effectiveness. For instance, 360-degree feedback systems, where input is gathered from various stakeholders, can provide valuable insights into a leader's performance and areas for improvement.

Ultimately, inviting feedback and critique is a hallmark of humble leadership. By fostering an environment where open dialogue is encouraged, Modeling receptiveness, and actively responding to input, leaders can enhance their effectiveness and drive organizational growth. This practice not only contributes to personal development but also cultivates a culture of collaboration and continuous learning within the team.

9.5 Humility and Long-Term Success

Humility, when practiced effectively by leaders, can significantly contribute to long-term organizational success. Unlike fleeting traits that may come and go, the consistent application of humility creates a lasting impact on workplace culture, employee engagement, and overall performance. This section explores how humility contributes to sustainable success and the key practices leaders can adopt to ensure it is embedded within their organizations.

One of the primary ways humilities foster long-term success is by cultivating strong relationships within teams. Leaders who demonstrate humility tend to build trust, as their openness encourages team members to engage authentically. This trust is foundational for collaboration, enabling teams to work together more effectively toward common goals. For instance, a humble leader who actively listens and values the opinions of their team creates a supportive atmosphere where individuals feel respected and empowered. Such an environment not only enhances teamwork but also promotes employee loyalty, reducing turnover and fostering a culture of retention.

Furthermore, humility enhances a leader's ability to adapt to change. In today's dynamic business environment, the capacity to pivot and embrace new ideas is crucial for survival. Humble leaders are more likely to seek input from their teams, recognizing that diverse perspectives can lead to innovative solutions. By valuing the contributions of others, they can harness collective intelligence to navigate challenges effectively. For example, during a significant organizational shift, a humble leader may invite insights from team members across different departments, fostering a collaborative approach to adaptation that leads to more effective outcomes.

In addition to fostering relationships and adaptability, humility is linked to ethical decision-making. Humble leaders are often more attuned to the values and well-being of their employees, which influences their decision-making processes. They are less likely to prioritize personal gain over the collective good and are more inclined to consider the long-term consequences of their actions. This ethical grounding is crucial for maintaining a positive reputation and ensuring organizational sustainability. Employees are more likely to remain engaged and committed to a leader who consistently prioritizes integrity and the welfare of the team over short-term results.

Moreover, humility encourages a learning-oriented culture within organizations. When leaders openly acknowledge their limitations and express a commitment to continuous improvement, they set a powerful example for their teams. This commitment fosters a culture where employees feel encouraged to take risks, learn from their mistakes, and pursue personal and professional growth. In such an environment, innovation flourishes, and the organization becomes more resilient in the face of challenges. Leaders who promote lifelong learning and development contribute to the overall success of their teams and organizations.

In conclusion, humility is a vital component of long-term success in leadership. By fostering strong relationships, enhancing adaptability, promoting ethical decision-making, and cultivating a learning-oriented culture, humble leaders can drive sustainable growth and success within their organizations. Embracing humility not only enhances a leader's effectiveness but also sets the stage for a thriving workplace where individuals feel valued, engaged, and inspired to contribute their best efforts.

10. Integrity

> *"Integrity is doing the right thing, even when no one is watching."* — C.S. Lewis

Integrity is the cornerstone of effective leadership, serving as the foundation upon which trust is built. In a world where leaders are often scrutinized for their decisions and actions, demonstrating integrity is essential for fostering a positive organizational culture and maintaining strong relationships with team members. This chapter explores the multifaceted nature of integrity in leadership, highlighting its significance and offering strategies for leaders to embody this vital trait.

10.1 Defining Integrity in Leadership

At its core, integrity involves adhering to a set of moral and ethical principles, and in the context of leadership, it means consistently aligning one's actions with these values. Leaders with integrity are transparent, honest, and fair in their dealings, earning the respect and trust of their teams. The definition of integrity extends beyond mere compliance with rules and regulations; it encompasses a commitment to ethical behaviour and accountability.

Integrity in leadership is not only about making the right choices but also about being accountable for those choices. When leaders act with integrity, they demonstrate a commitment to their values, which can significantly influence the organizational culture. For example, a leader who prioritizes honesty and transparency in their communications encourages team members to do the same, creating an environment where ethical behaviour is the norm. This fosters a culture of trust, where employees feel secure in expressing their ideas and concerns without fear of retaliation.

Moreover, leaders with integrity are often seen as role models by their teams. Their consistent ethical behaviour sets a standard for others to follow, reinforcing the importance of integrity within the organization. For instance, when leaders acknowledge their mistakes and take responsibility for their actions, it sends a powerful message to employees that accountability is valued. This transparency not only enhances the leader's credibility but also empowers team members to take ownership of their actions, fostering a culture of responsibility.

10.2 Leading with Transparency

Transparency is a critical aspect of integrity in leadership. When leaders communicate openly and honestly, they build trust and create an environment where team members feel informed and valued. Transparency involves sharing relevant information, explaining decision-making processes, and being candid about challenges and successes. This open communication fosters a sense of belonging and engagement among employees, encouraging them to contribute their insights and perspectives.

A transparent leader provides clarity regarding organizational goals and objectives, ensuring that team members understand how their roles contribute to the bigger picture. This understanding enhances employee motivation and alignment with organizational values. For example, when a leader shares the rationale behind a significant organizational change, it helps team members grasp the context and purpose, reducing uncertainty and resistance.

Additionally, leaders should practice transparency in acknowledging their limitations and areas for improvement. By openly discussing challenges and inviting feedback, leaders demonstrate humility and a willingness to grow. This approach not only builds trust but also encourages team members to voice their concerns and suggestions. A culture of transparency empowers employees to speak up and take initiative, ultimately leading to improved collaboration and innovation.

In conclusion, integrity is a fundamental quality for effective leadership, encompassing ethical behaviour, accountability, and transparency. Leaders who embody integrity set the tone for their organizations, fostering a culture of trust and collaboration. By defining integrity in leadership and prioritizing transparency, leaders can create an environment where ethical behaviour thrives, contributing to long-term success and a positive organizational culture.

10.3 Ethics and Decision-Making

Ethics plays a critical role in decision-making processes for leaders, guiding their actions and influencing the overall direction of the organization. In essence, ethical decision-making involves evaluating choices based on moral principles and values, rather than merely considering outcomes or personal gain. Leaders who prioritize ethics in their decision-making not only uphold their integrity but also set a strong ethical framework for their organizations.

A significant aspect of ethical decision-making is the recognition of the broader impact of choices. Leaders must consider how their decisions affect not only their team members but also stakeholders, customers, and the community at large. This holistic approach promotes accountability and demonstrates that leaders are mindful of their responsibilities. For instance, a leader facing a budget cut must weigh the immediate financial benefits against the potential negative effects on employee morale and job security. An ethical leader would prioritize transparency in communicating these challenges and seek input from team members before making a final decision.

Furthermore, leaders should establish a clear ethical framework within their organizations to guide decision-making processes. This framework can include a code of ethics, which outlines the values and principles that employees are expected to uphold. By integrating these ethical guidelines into the decision-making process, leaders can foster a culture of accountability and trust. Employees are more likely to feel empowered to voice their opinions and concerns when they understand the ethical standards guiding their organization.

An essential tool for ethical decision-making is the practice of ethical reasoning. Leaders can employ various ethical frameworks, such as utilitarianism, deontology, or virtue ethics, to evaluate their choices. For example, a leader might apply utilitarian principles by considering the greatest good for the greatest number when faced with a challenging decision. Alternatively, a deontological approach would focus on the adherence to moral duties and obligations, regardless of the consequences. By applying these frameworks, leaders can ensure that their decisions align with their core values and the organization's ethical standards.

Moreover, it is crucial for leaders to engage in ongoing ethical reflection. This involves regularly assessing their values, the decisions they make, and the potential consequences of those choices. By fostering a mindset of ethical reflection, leaders can enhance their self-awareness and reinforce their commitment to integrity. This practice not only strengthens their decision-making skills but also sets a powerful example for their teams, encouraging a culture of ethical consideration throughout the organization.

In summary, ethics and decision-making are closely intertwined, with integrity serving as the guiding force. Leaders who prioritize ethical decision-making not only uphold their own integrity but also contribute to a culture of accountability and trust within their organizations. By establishing ethical frameworks, employing ethical reasoning, and engaging in ongoing reflection, leaders can navigate complex decisions with confidence and align their actions with their values.

10.4 Addressing Conflicts with Integrity

In any organization, conflicts are inevitable. How leaders handle these conflicts can significantly impact their credibility and the overall health of the workplace culture. Addressing conflicts with integrity involves approaching the situation transparently, honestly, and fairly, ensuring that all parties feel heard and respected. This chapter delves into the strategies leaders can employ to manage conflicts while upholding their integrity.

One of the first steps in addressing conflicts with integrity is acknowledging the issue openly. Ignoring conflicts or allowing them to fester can lead to a toxic work environment and diminish trust among team members. Leaders must be proactive in identifying conflicts and addressing them directly. For example, if a disagreement arises between team members over a project approach, a leader should facilitate a meeting to discuss the differing viewpoints. This not only shows that the leader values open communication but also encourages a collaborative problem-solving approach.

In the conflict resolution process, active listening plays a vital role. Leaders must listen attentively to all parties involved, seeking to understand their perspectives and underlying concerns. By demonstrating empathy and a willingness to engage in dialogue, leaders create an atmosphere where team members feel safe to express their feelings and opinions. This approach not only helps to de-escalate tensions but also fosters a sense of trust and respect among team members.

Moreover, leaders should strive for fairness in conflict resolution. This means making decisions based on objective criteria rather than personal biases or emotions. When leaders are perceived as fair, it reinforces their integrity and builds confidence in their leadership. For instance, if a conflict arises over workload distribution, a leader should evaluate the situation based on measurable performance metrics and team needs, rather than favouritism. Transparent communication of the decision-making process can further enhance perceptions of fairness.

Another essential aspect of addressing conflicts with integrity is the commitment to finding a resolution that is acceptable to all parties. Leaders should aim for win-win outcomes, where the solution addresses the core concerns of those involved while aligning with organizational goals. This may require compromise and negotiation skills, but it is crucial for maintaining trust and cooperation. For example, if two team members disagree on project priorities, a leader might facilitate a brainstorming session to identify a solution that incorporates both perspectives.

In conclusion, addressing conflicts with integrity is crucial for maintaining a healthy organizational culture and fostering trust among team members. By openly acknowledging conflicts, practicing active listening, ensuring fairness, and striving for collaborative resolutions, leaders can navigate challenges effectively while reinforcing their integrity. This commitment not only enhances their credibility as leaders but also contributes to a more resilient and cohesive team.

10.5 Integrity as a Foundation for Culture

Integrity serves as the cornerstone of an organization's culture, shaping the values and behaviours that define how team members interact and collaborate. A strong foundation of integrity fosters trust, respect, and accountability, which are essential for a thriving workplace. This chapter explores how leaders can cultivate a culture of integrity within their organizations and the long-term benefits that arise from such an environment.

To begin with, leaders must model integrity in their actions. When leaders consistently demonstrate ethical behaviour, they set the standard for their teams. This modelling creates a ripple effect, encouraging employees to adopt similar values in their own work. For instance, if a leader openly discusses the importance of ethical decision-making and exemplifies it in their actions, team members are more likely to embrace these principles in their day-to-day responsibilities. This alignment between leaders and employees strengthens the organization's moral compass, guiding behaviours toward integrity.

Furthermore, leaders should establish clear values and expectations that reinforce integrity as a core principle. This can be achieved through the creation of a formal code of ethics, which outlines the organization's commitment to ethical conduct and provides guidance on navigating complex situations. When employees understand the ethical standards expected of them, they are more likely to engage in behaviours that reflect integrity.

For example, regular training sessions on ethical dilemmas can enhance employees' understanding of how to apply integrity in their roles, ultimately contributing to a cohesive culture.

Another crucial aspect of fostering a culture of integrity is recognizing and rewarding ethical behaviour. Leaders should celebrate instances of integrity within their teams, whether through formal recognition programs or informal acknowledgment. By highlighting positive examples of ethical conduct, leaders reinforce the message that integrity is valued and appreciated within the organization. This recognition not only motivates individuals to act ethically but also cultivates an environment where ethical behaviour is normalized.

Additionally, leaders must be prepared to address unethical behaviour promptly and decisively. Ignoring or tolerating unethical actions undermines the organization's commitment to integrity and can lead to a toxic culture. When employees observe leaders addressing unethical behaviour transparently, it strengthens the belief that integrity is a priority. For instance, if an employee is found engaging in dishonest practices, leaders must take appropriate action, demonstrating that ethical standards are non-negotiable. This proactive approach reinforces a culture where integrity is paramount.

In summary, integrity is a foundational element of organizational culture, influencing how employees interact, make decisions, and approach their work. By modelling integrity, establishing clear values, recognizing ethical behaviour, and addressing unethical actions, leaders can cultivate a culture where integrity thrives. This commitment not only enhances the organization's reputation but also contributes to long-term success, employee engagement, and a positive workplace environment.

11. Passion

> *"The only way to do great work is to love what you do."* * — *Steve Jobs*

P assion is the fuel that drives effective leadership, inspiring individuals and teams to pursue excellence in their endeavours. A leader's enthusiasm and commitment can ignite a sense of purpose among team members, fostering an environment where creativity and innovation flourish. This chapter will explore the significance of passion in leadership, how leaders can cultivate their own passion, and strategies to inspire passion within their teams.

11.1 The Influence of Passion in Leadership

Passion is a powerful motivator, not just for leaders themselves but for everyone within an organization. Leaders who exhibit genuine passion for their work tend to engage their teams more effectively, as enthusiasm is contagious. When leaders communicate their vision with energy and conviction, it resonates with team members, encouraging them to connect personally with their roles and the organization's mission. For instance, a passionate leader who articulates a clear and compelling vision for a project can inspire their team to go above and beyond in their contributions, leading to heightened performance and creativity.

Moreover, passionate leaders are often more resilient in the face of challenges. Their deep commitment to their goals fuels perseverance, allowing them to navigate setbacks with optimism and determination. This resilience not only sets a positive example for team members but also encourages a culture where challenges are viewed as opportunities for growth rather than insurmountable obstacles. For example, during a difficult project, a passionate leader might rally their team by focusing on the shared purpose and the positive impact their work will have, thereby motivating them to push through adversity.

11.2 Staying Motivated as a Leader

To harness the power of passion effectively, leaders must cultivate and maintain their own motivation. This requires self-awareness and a commitment to personal development. Leaders should regularly reflect on their goals, values, and the impact they wish to have, ensuring that their work remains aligned with their passions. Engaging in activities that inspire creativity and enthusiasm, such as attending workshops, networking with like-minded individuals, or exploring new ideas, can rejuvenate a leader's spirit and keep their passion alive.

Additionally, leaders should seek feedback from their teams to understand how their passion and motivation resonate with others. Open discussions about team dynamics and individual aspirations can provide valuable insights, allowing leaders to adjust their approaches and maintain alignment with the team's collective goals. By fostering an environment of open communication, leaders can ensure that their passion becomes a shared journey rather than a solitary pursuit.

Furthermore, setting clear and meaningful goals can help leaders maintain their motivation. When leaders establish specific, measurable objectives that are aligned with their passions, they create a sense of purpose and direction. Regularly revisiting these goals and celebrating milestones can keep the fire of passion burning strong. For instance, recognizing team achievements and sharing success stories can reinforce a sense of accomplishment, further fuelling collective passion and commitment to the organization's mission.

11.3 Inspiring Passion in Your Team

Inspiring passion within a team is crucial for creating an energized and engaged workforce. As a leader, your ability to motivate and empower team members can significantly enhance their performance and satisfaction. This section will discuss various strategies that leaders can employ to inspire passion among their teams.

One of the most effective ways to ignite passion is through shared purpose. When team members understand how their work contributes to the larger mission of the organization, they are more likely to feel a sense of ownership and commitment. Leaders should clearly articulate the organization's vision and mission, ensuring that each team member understands their role in achieving these goals. For example, a leader might hold a meeting to discuss the organization's objectives and explain how each team member's contributions directly impact those goals. This connection fosters a sense of belonging and motivates team members to invest their energy and creativity into their work.

Additionally, encouraging autonomy and creativity can significantly enhance passion within the team. When employees are given the freedom to make decisions and explore innovative solutions, they are more likely to feel engaged and passionate about their work. Leaders should create an environment that supports experimentation, where team members feel comfortable sharing their ideas without fear of criticism. For instance, a leader might implement a brainstorming session where all ideas are welcomed and considered, regardless of their feasibility. This inclusive approach can lead to groundbreaking solutions and ignite enthusiasm within the team.

Recognizing and celebrating achievements is another vital component of inspiring passion. Leaders should regularly acknowledge both individual and team successes, no matter how small. This recognition fosters a positive atmosphere and reinforces the value of hard work and dedication. Celebrating milestones can be as simple as a shout-out in team meetings or as elaborate as hosting a team event to commemorate significant accomplishments. This practice not only boosts morale but also reinforces the idea that passion and effort lead to success.

Furthermore, fostering a culture of continuous learning and development can enhance team members' passion. Leaders should encourage employees to pursue professional development opportunities, such as workshops, courses, or mentorship programs. Providing resources for skill enhancement not only helps individuals grow but also contributes to the overall capabilities of the team. Leaders can inspire passion by sharing their own learning journeys and emphasizing the importance of lifelong learning. When team members see their leader actively pursuing growth, it motivates them to do the same.

In summary, inspiring passion in a team requires leaders to create a shared purpose, encourage autonomy, recognize achievements, and promote continuous learning. By implementing these strategies, leaders can cultivate a motivated and engaged workforce, resulting in enhanced performance, creativity, and satisfaction.

11.4 Sustaining Passion Through Challenges

Maintaining passion during difficult times is crucial for effective leadership and team cohesion. Challenges are an inevitable part of any organizational journey, and how leaders respond to these challenges can significantly influence the morale and motivation of their teams. This section will explore strategies for sustaining passion through adversity.

First, it's essential for leaders to foster a supportive environment during challenging times. When teams face obstacles, leaders should prioritize open communication and transparency. Keeping lines of communication open helps team members feel valued and supported, and it allows them to express their concerns and ideas. For instance, a leader might hold regular check-ins to discuss progress, address challenges, and provide reassurance. This proactive approach not only alleviates stress but also reinforces the sense that everyone is in the journey together.

Moreover, leaders can reframe challenges as opportunities for growth. By adopting a positive mindset, leaders can inspire their teams to view obstacles as chances to learn and develop. This reframing encourages resilience and creativity, allowing team members to explore new solutions rather than becoming overwhelmed by setbacks. For example, a leader might share personal stories of overcoming challenges, highlighting the lessons learned and the eventual successes that followed. Such narratives can serve as powerful reminders that passion and perseverance often lead to rewarding outcomes.

Another key strategy is to set short-term goals during challenging periods. Long-term objectives can feel daunting when faced with significant hurdles, leading to feelings of discouragement. By breaking down larger goals into smaller, achievable milestones, leaders can help their teams maintain focus and motivation. Celebrating the completion of these smaller goals reinforces a sense of accomplishment and keeps the passion alive, even in tough times. For instance, a project manager might set weekly targets for their team, celebrating each achievement to maintain momentum and enthusiasm.

Additionally, providing opportunities for team bonding and morale-boosting activities can help sustain passion during challenging periods. Engaging in team-building exercises or social events allows team members to connect on a personal level, strengthening relationships and fostering a sense of community. A leader might organize informal gatherings, virtual coffee breaks, or team challenges to encourage camaraderie and alleviate stress. Such activities can reignite passion and motivation, reminding team members that they are part of a supportive unit.

In summary, sustaining passion through challenges requires leaders to foster a supportive environment, reframe challenges as opportunities, set achievable goals, and promote team bonding. By implementing these strategies, leaders can help their teams navigate difficulties with resilience and maintain their passion for achieving the organization's objectives.

11.5 Balancing Passion with Practicality

While passion is a vital component of effective leadership, it must be balanced with practicality to ensure sustainable success. Leaders who are overly passionate without a grounded approach may overlook critical aspects of decision-making, strategic planning, and resource management. This section will discuss strategies for maintaining this balance, ensuring that enthusiasm translates into productive outcomes.

One of the first steps in achieving this balance is to establish clear priorities and objectives. Passion can sometimes lead to enthusiasm for multiple projects or initiatives, which can scatter focus and resources. Leaders should take the time to identify and communicate the organization's top priorities, ensuring that passion is directed towards achieving these goals. For example, a leader might conduct a strategic planning session to determine which projects align best with the organization's mission and available resources. This focused approach allows team members to channel their passion effectively, maximizing their contributions toward the most critical objectives.

Moreover, leaders should foster a culture of data-driven decision-making. While passion is important, it must be supported by solid evidence and analysis to drive effective outcomes. Leaders should encourage their teams to utilize data and metrics to evaluate progress and inform decisions. For instance, before launching a new initiative, a leader might ask the team to conduct market research, assess potential risks, and analyze expected outcomes based on historical data. This practice not only enhances the credibility of decisions but also ensures that passion is directed towards strategies that are feasible and beneficial.

In addition, leaders must practice flexibility and adaptability. The business landscape is constantly changing, and rigid adherence to passion-driven plans can lead to failure if circumstances shift. Leaders should remain open to new information and be willing to adjust their strategies as needed. For example, if a previously popular product begins to decline in sales, a passionate leader should be willing to pivot the focus of the team to explore new opportunities rather than stubbornly sticking to an outdated plan. This adaptability not only protects the organization's interests but also demonstrates a pragmatic approach to leadership.

Finally, it's crucial for leaders to communicate openly with their teams about the balance between passion and practicality. Regular discussions about priorities, goals, and challenges can help teams understand the rationale behind decisions. By fostering an environment where team members feel comfortable sharing their thoughts, leaders can harness the collective passion of the group while ensuring that practical considerations are not overlooked. For instance, a leader might implement a feedback loop where team members can voice their ideas and concerns, contributing to a collaborative decision-making process.

In summary, balancing passion with practicality requires leaders to establish clear priorities, utilize data-driven decision-making, practice flexibility, and communicate openly with their teams. By achieving this balance, leaders can inspire passion while ensuring that enthusiasm translates into meaningful and sustainable results.

12. Conclusion: Embracing the Journey of Leadership

As we reach the conclusion of "LEADERSHIP: Lessons for Lasting Impact," it's vital to reflect on the key themes and insights discussed throughout this book. Leadership is not just a title or position; it is a continuous journey of growth, learning, and influence. The principles outlined in the chapters—Listening, Empathy, Accountability, Decisiveness, Empowerment, Resilience, Strategy, Humility, Integrity, and Passion—serve as the foundational pillars for effective leadership. Each chapter has provided actionable insights, strategies, and real-world examples to empower leaders at all levels.

Leadership requires active listening to understand the needs and concerns of team members, which fosters a culture of trust and open communication. Empathy enables leaders to connect with their teams on a human level, paving the way for collaboration and understanding. The emphasis on accountability highlights the importance of taking responsibility for one's actions and decisions, creating a culture where everyone feels empowered to contribute.

Moreover, decisiveness is essential for making timely and informed choices, especially in a fast-paced business environment. Leaders must also recognize the significance of empowerment, inspiring their teams to excel and take ownership of their roles. The discussions around resilience remind us that setbacks are inevitable, but with a strong mindset, they can be transformed into opportunities for growth.

Developing a strategic vision is critical for guiding teams toward shared goals. A leader's humility allows for a culture of learning, where feedback is embraced and mistakes are viewed as stepping stones rather than failures. Integrity builds trust within the team and establishes a strong ethical foundation for decision-making. Lastly, fostering passion ensures that enthusiasm and commitment are woven into the fabric of the organization, motivating team members to strive for excellence.

In conclusion, effective leadership is a dynamic interplay of these elements, requiring a delicate balance between passion and practicality. As you embark on your leadership journey, remember that growth comes from continuous learning and adaptation. Embrace the challenges, celebrate the successes, and remain committed to inspiring those around you. The impact of your leadership will extend beyond your immediate circle, influencing future generations and shaping a better world.

As you implement the lessons learned in this book, strive to be the leader who not only achieves results but also inspires others to reach their full potential. Leadership is a privilege, and with it comes the responsibility to leave a lasting impact on your organization and the people you serve. Keep pushing forward, and remember that every step you take in your leadership journey contributes to a legacy of excellence.

www.ingramcontent.com/pod-product-compliance
Lightning Source LLC
Chambersburg PA
CBHW070115230526
45472CB00004B/1264